Finding Margin for the Devotional Life

Finding Margin for the Devotional Life

Shellie Rushing Tomlinson

Ripples from Providence

CONTENTS

Introduction

I jumped on social media a while back to ask my listeners to help me help them by weighing in on what they would like me to speak about in future episodes of my podcast. The choices were,

1. How to develop a prayer life from scratch, B) Where to begin if you're new to Bible study, or C) How to find devotional time when you already feel stretched too thin.

The level of response was as surprising as the variety of votes. There was no consensus. Seeing as those responding were expressing interest in all three topics, I decided to take turns addressing each of them. What follows is intentionally brief because, again, the issue addressed is creating margin in a world short on time and starved for meaning.

Hugs,
Shellie

How to Find Time for a Devotional Life When You Already Feel Stretched Too Thin

Allow me to preface this big subject with an acknowledgment. People the world over are living in myriad circumstances and facing a variety of experiences—many with unique time demands I haven't encountered. I offer that as an uncontested fact. At the same time, I hold to the following rock-solid belief built on the authority of God's Word. Anyone who endeavors to know God and refuses to settle for anything less will always run into God's divine intention to be known. Call it God's set-up for success.

You will seek Me and find Me when you search for Me with all your heart. Jeremiah 29:13

That's not simply an encouraging verse or me reaching for a handy disclaimer. It's foundational truth for a conversation on finding devotional time. None of us can make time or find time. The best we can do is manage it. So, with that established, we'll frame our discussion with the language of finding and losing because it's easy to understand. No doubt you've heard the old axiom, "We make time for what matters." It's true.

All serious conversations about developing a devotional life begin here, with our priorities. What lengths are we willing to take to walk closely with God? What sacrifices will me make? How much do we want such a life? I fear that for most of us, finding margin in our schedules for God must be easy, convenient, and immediately rewarding, lest we grow weary and faint far short of the goal.

Can we come to Christ in a second? Yes, and amen. Can He redeem us from a world of sin and make us His instantaneously, sealed forever by His Spirit? Absolutely. But we'll never come to know Him intimately in that same way, and any claims to the contrary are biblically unfounded.

For the remainder of this particular conversation, I'd like to assume we've all counted the cost, and we've decided knowing the One who made us, redeemed us, and is coming back for us is worth whatever lifestyle sacrifice is required. Let's say we've realized we won't fall into such a relationship with Jesus accidentally or automatically, and we're here for the long haul, but our days are still maxed out, our time does not feel like our own, and we don't see margins anywhere. What now?

May I humbly suggest that the best way forward is a change of perspective?

I heartily recommend aiming for a devoted life over a devotional life. Again, I'm not mincing words or trying to be cute. I'm hoping to shed light on attitudes that often trip us up, and a devotional life can sometimes suggest a certain part of our day, whereas a devoted life pictures someone in ongoing pursuit of Jesus.

A devotional life may have a certain time of day in mind where we intend to read or pray, and if we miss that time, so be it until the next regularly scheduled opportunity. A devoted life is always looking to feed on the Word and listen for God's voice, whether in prayer, in the company of others, or in the sights and sounds of nature.

"Having a devotional" is contained in time and place. Someone living a devoted life will listen to the audio Bible or a teaching podcast while she gets in her steps at the gym, while she's stuck in traffic, or when she's waiting to pick her child up from ball practice. Will she have to say no to the countless other mindless temptations to escape through a few scrolls of her smart phone?

Yes, but remember, she's committed and aware that having a devotional is a once-a-day endeavor, and she wants the rewards of a devoted life.

Those who live devoted are always on the lookout for snatches of time to nourish their souls, however small those moments may be at first. But as those moments begin to transform their days, they find themselves increasingly aware that they're looking for more places and previously unrealized opportunities to feed themselves.

If you'll allow me a moment of personal testimony? This change in attitude toward being devoted rather than having a devotional changed my life years ago, and God continues to use it transform my life today. If it speaks to you and if it sets you on a different type of pursuit of God than you've ever been on before, I'd like to ask you to let me know so I can pray for you, by name. You'll find ways to contact me at the end of this little book.

How and Where to Begin if You're New to Bible Study

It's not hard to remember the days when I wanted to love the Bible, but I just flat-out didn't, and trying to read it made me sleepy. So, let's start there.

If you're new to the Bible, or even if you're not that new to it but you've never developed a hunger for digging into it on your own, my first suggestion is for you to take your current experience with the Bible, whatever that looks like, and approach God with it in prayer. Ask Him to help you develop a desire for His Word and to teach you through it—and then ask Him again tomorrow. I still pray this way on an ongoing basis. I thank God that His Word has become as much bread to me as the physical food I eat. I acknowledge that He has done this marvelous thing, not me, and I ask Him to help me love His Word more than I did yesterday. He is faithful.

My second suggestion is one you'll find in a lot of places that address this question. That's because it is solid good advice, and why reinvent the wheel, right? Find a translation that you can understand. A few of my favorites are the New American Standard Bible, the English Standard Version, the New International Version, the Revised Standard Version, the Amplified and the Holman Christian Standard Bible. Okay, that was more than a few, but you get the idea.

If you can't buy a Bible just now, type a verse in on a search engine and you'll find websites where you can read a slew of different translations as quickly as your Internet can load the page, all free. Take every advantage of that. Reading the same verse in various translations will often open our eyes to something we didn't see in the initial reading.

To recap: begin by asking God to help you love His Word, and then find a translation you can understand. The third suggestion brings us right down to the meat of this discussion. I'm often asked where to begin reading and how much to read? For me, both of those questions require me to assume an uncomfortable level of authority, but I'm game to answer if you will take my thoughts as just that, my thoughts. There are as many answers as there are Bible teachers.

That being said, I like to direct new Bible students to John's gospel. That's the fourth book of the New Testament. The gospel of John is beautiful, profound reading. This is going to be a real oversimplification, but where the first three gospel writers major on the humanity of Jesus and the timeline of His earthly ministry, John's first words take us all the way back to the beginning: "In the beginning was the Word, and the Word was with God." John opens with the divinity of Jesus as the living Word of God who first spoke the world into existence, and then devotes his efforts to establishing this same Jesus as the Son of God and long-awaited long-promised Savior, stepping into time to redeem it. John's gospel is my favorite because He stresses the importance of the lordship of Jesus and our need to believe and keep believing. That speaks to this remedial learner who totally gets the words of the anxious daddy in the gospel accounts who once said,

"Lord, I believe. Help my unbelief!" Approach the book of John in bites—not to conquer the reading, but to hear the words. (If you want to walk with me through John, look for my Bible study *Seizing the Good Life* wherever books are sold.)

Also, don't try to read too much at one sitting unless you're drawn forward. For instance, the first verse of the first chapter is weighty and full of glory, and the chapter has another fifty verses! Pace yourself. The first five verses are a manageable section by themselves. Take them one or two at a time, but don't race. Read and savor. Pause and ponder. Ask the Holy Spirit to talk to you about what you're reading and to help you take His words into your day. If you want to do more, type that verse into a search engine along with the word "commentary," and read what other learned scholars have to say about it. Whatever time you give to unpacking that verse will be to your great benefit.

But let's back up even further. Let's say the idea of studying a book seems too much to you. You can always start with a good devotional. Most of the daily readings will include a Scripture verse. Acknowledge to God in prayer that you know those biblical words are more important than anything the devotional author said and ask Him to teach you more about them. Say the verse aloud, write it down, or peck it out in a notepad on your smart phone. Meditate on the words. The truth you pull from them will belong to you and to your descendants forever!

See what I just did there? I quoted Scripture and I didn't have to reach for it. Holy Spirit brought the words of Deuteronomy 29:29 back to me because I've often held that promise to my heart. "The secret things belong to the Lord, but the things revealed belong to us and to our descendants forever."

The more you engage with God's Word, the more of it you'll remember too, and God will be able to bring it back to your thoughts during the day and speak to you through it.

We'll end with another delicious truth: If you engage with God's living Word, God's living Words will engage you.

That's my oh so simple recap on getting into God's Word. Walk with me at ShellieT.com for an ongoing discussion. I hope these brief thoughts have helped you. It's fun for me to think about and trace the steps that led to my love of God's Word! For instance, right now, it's occurring to me that listening to teaching podcasts has been another tool the Lord has used to stir up my hunger for His Word, so offering you whatever help I can through mine feels really cool to me! Let's turn our thoughts towards prayer.

How to Develop a Prayer Life from Scratch

Honestly, it's hard to know where to begin on this topic, but not for the reason you might think. I have plenty to say on the subject! Prayer has become such a valuable way of life to me that I could easily go on and on—but therein lies the challenge. I don't want to ramble. I want to be clear and concise so I can be of help to you instead of just one more voice in a world of nonstop noise.

In so many ways, I wish I could wrap up my prayer life and hand it to anyone who desires to walk with God. Hear me, I don't believe it had to be as hard as it was or take as long as it did for me to learn how to enjoy prayer. But the fact remains, it was hard, and it didn't happen overnight. I'm hoping to identify the obstacles that held me back, with the humble goal that I might make your road easier. And I know right where I want to start!

I just lowered my eyes and asked Holy Spirit to give me wisdom and help me articulate these thoughts well. And then, I almost giggled because this the most obvious prayer suggestion I could ever give you, and yet, it's a necessary step I was very slow to recognize in my own prayer life, and one I could have easily forgotten to share. I'm so glad He nudged me to tell you. My first suggestion, when you go to prayer, is simply that:

1. **Ask the Holy Spirit to help you pray.**
   Just as we need the Spirit's help in understanding the Word, as surely as we need the Spirit's indwelling strength to daily walk

out God's will for our lives, we need the Spirit's help to pray.

Start there.

2. **Always go to God through Jesus.**

That's my second suggestion. Learn the immense value of preaching the Gospel to yourself when you bow to pray. Maybe other people don't need to do this as often as the believer talking to you, but I'm hoping to communicate as openly as possible, as this is my experience.

It doesn't matter how long it's been since I've sat in prayer—sometimes I can want to pray, I can need to pray, and God still feels a million miles away. I treasure the lesson of the Holy Spirit here and how He has taught me to position myself on the solid foundation of God's love for me instead of trusting in my love for God. I remind myself that my impassioned prayers don't give me more access to God's throne, and any temporary dryness on my part doesn't bar me from it. I wish I could always bring Him a flaming heart, but when I can't, I can always trust Him to be near, and to hear, because of Jesus. Our access to His throne isn't our emotional state or our current situation. It is Jesus. All Jesus.

Far be it from me to dictate words anyone else should use, but simply to make this clearer, here's a sample of how I might open a prayer time using the first two suggestions. It may sound something like this: *Father, thank You that You hear me because of Jesus. And Jesus, thank You for the sacrifice that reconciled me to Your Father and mine. Holy Spirit, help me pray.* Of course, there are all kinds of words I might use to express this. I'm simply advocating the principles.

As I noted earlier, this is a topic I could talk about at length and still not feel like I touched it. I'm hoping, Good Lord willing, to write a more in-depth book on prayer. My plan is to write it with enough self-effacing humor at all my hits and misses that my reader will realize I'm no expert, just a woman in love with Jesus who wants to share the journey.

For now, I'll leave you with a reminder, and a final suggestion. Here's the reminder. The One who said, "Be still, and know that I am God" is willing to teach us how to talk to Him and listen for Him. Let that encourage us as we learn to quiet ourselves before Him.

And now, my closing suggestion.

3. Bring your wandering thoughts to God, too!

I'll explain. My brain can think of a thousand and one hundred things in the time it can take me to express one coherent prayer to God. If this isn't your experience, bless you. Give thanks.

If it does happen to you, ask Holy Spirit to unite your heart and mind. Ask Him to show you if any of the circling thoughts require confession on your part, and if you're prompted to repent, tend to it quickly. Sometimes, when we're praying and trying to ignore a persistent thought, the persistent thought can be precisely what Holy Spirit is moving us to pray about. If it's not a matter of sin in your own life, ask for wisdom, comfort, strength, whatever you need to address the issue— and then listen.

Granted, that's not always the case. Sometimes my brain is offering up deep theological suggestions like—oh, I don't know, the importance of picking up black pepper at the store, not salt, because I've picked it up three times straight, but pepper, Shellie, pepper, pepper, pepper!

I've found it hugely helpful to stop and jot down random notes that won't go away. (I love to use the notepad app on my phone for this!) Many times, jotting something down tends to put it to rest in my head so I can continue to pray.

And that reminds me of one more thing. (Sorry. I guess there will be four tips, which makes me want to do five because I like odd numbers, and if you're still there, pray for me. That was a joke. Kind of.) To my point, don't let yourself be frustrated when your thoughts wander during prayer, and don't let yourself be so overtaken with guilt that you quit praying. Why do I say this?

Because I've done both. Tip Four is bigger than it seems:

4. When your mind does wander, simply bring it back.

That's right. Don't feel guilty. Don't be frustrated and don't quit. Just ask the Holy Spirit to help your mind to focus and bring it back. If you have to bring it back once, twice, or a hundred times, do it. God will meet you in your commitment.

That's it for now. Come find me at ShellieT.com and subscribe to say in touch. Oh, and invite your friends to join us and share the journey. He is worthy.

Hugs,
Shellie

You can reach me at <u>writeshellie@gmail.com</u> and through my *Facebook*, *Instagram*, and *Twitter* accounts. I respond as promptly as possible.